This book is dedicated to my daughters,
Laura and Emma, with love.

OUT AND ABOUT
Wild Flowers
Discovering British

Deirdre A. Shirreffs

Brambleby Books

I thank Margaret Alston, and Julie Newman, both primary school teachers, and Dr. Peter Llewellyn for their valuable input and suggestions, and the latter also for his images on pages 41, 65, 72 & 93 marked ©PL; and Dr. Richard Harrington for the bee image on page 10.

Contents

Introduction ... 6
Symbols ... 6
Parts of a Plant ... 7
Parts of a Flower ... 8
Pollination and Fertilisation ... 9
Seed Dispersal ... 10
Leaf Shapes ... 11
Flower Families ... 14
Scientific Names ... 17

Woodlands ... 19

Heaths and Moors ... 37

Walls ... 49

Dunes and Seashores ... 57

Marshes, Lakes and Rivers ... 65

Gardens and Parks ... 77

Hedgerows and Roadsides ... 87

Fields ... 123

Meadows and Grasslands ... 135

General and Plant Index ... 151

Flower Colour Index ... 154

Useful Websites ... 159

Introduction

Have you ever seen a Daisy on sand dunes, Poppies in a wood or Wood Anemones in a field? Probably not because every plant is adapted to its habitat, as with all wildlife. In this book you will find descriptions of over one hundred common British wild flowers arranged by the habitat they *usually* grow in (although some may grow in several). To identify plants by the colour of their flowers, check the photographic Flower Colour Index, page 154. When you find a flower you can tick the box at the bottom of the relevant page and make some notes. For each plant its average height, type of pollination and main flowering season is given.

Each plant description starts with the common name, followed by its scientific name and the family the plant belongs to. The three-sectioned description begins with a general part, the second describes the flowers, seeds and fruit, and the third the leaves and stem. You certainly should never try to eat a wild plant you don't know as some are poisonous and potentially deadly.

It is best not to pick wild flowers. Leave them growing for others to enjoy (also they might be poisonous). Better try to draw them or take a photo instead. Many smartphones have very good cameras and you can buy a clip-on macro lens for a few pounds. Remember to take the book to the plant to identify it and not the other way round. Actually, it is against the law to uproot a plant without the landowner's permission.

Symbols

(i) general information

🍀 flowers, seeds and fruit    leaves and stem

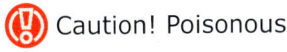 Caution! Poisonous!

 insect pollination

 spring

 autumn

 Height (cm or m)

 wind pollination

 summer

 winter

Parts of a plant

Flowering plants have a stem with leaves and flowers above ground. The leaves are green and use energy from sunlight to make the plant's food. They grow on stalks called petioles. The flower (or flowers) grows at the end of the stem. The roots grow in soil and anchor the plant. They form a network which absorbs water and nutrients from the soil. Some plants have a large, thick root called a tap root. The carrots you eat are just very large tap roots.

Parts of a flower

It is important to recognise the parts of a flower to be able to identify it. A buttercup is a good example of a flowering plant as it shows the flower parts clearly.

There are four parts to a typical flower – sepals, petals, stamens and pistil. These are best illustrated using a cross-section through a flower, as shown below.

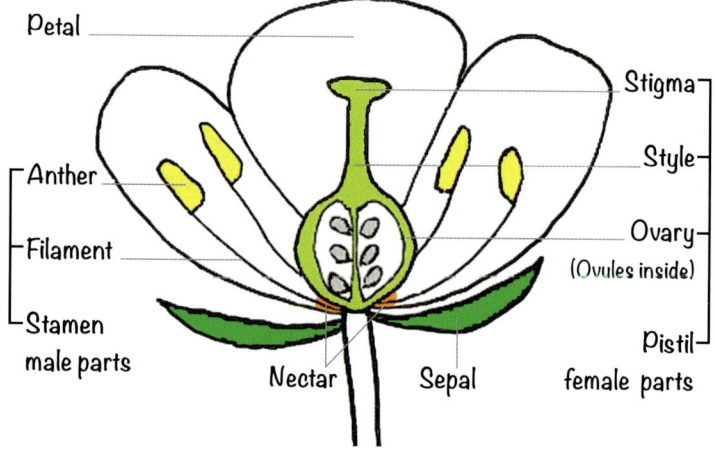

The **sepals** are green and protect the flower when it is in bud and then support the petals when the flower opens. They are also known as the calyx. They can be joined into a tube as in primroses and campions.

The **petals** are usually coloured, e.g. bright yellow in a buttercup, and showy to attract insect pollinators (see opposite). They sometimes have lines or spots on them to guide insects to their nectar reward – these are known as honey guides. Remember that bees see colour differently from us, so a flower that looks one colour to us may be very different to a bee's ultra-violet vision.

The **stamens** are the male part of the flower with **anthers** on **filaments** containing the **pollen**. They are often yellow but can be other colours. Poppies have black stamens for example.

The female part of the flower is the **pistil**, with the **ovary** in the centre of the flower and a **stigma** on the top of the **style** to catch the pollen. The ovary contains one or more **ovules** which develop into seeds when fertilised. Buttercups have many separate ovaries called **carpels**, each with one ovule.

Pollination and Fertilisation

For an ovule to develop into a seed two things need to happen – first pollination then fertilisation.

Pollination occurs when pollen (from the male flower parts) lands on the stigma (from the female parts). If pollen and stigma are on the same plant then the flower is self-pollinated (like tomatoes); however, most other plants only allow pollen from a different plant of the same kind; this is termed cross-pollination. In the next step, the pollen produces a tube to transfer its DNA (genetic material) downward to mix with the DNA of the ovule. This is now fertilised and will become a seed.

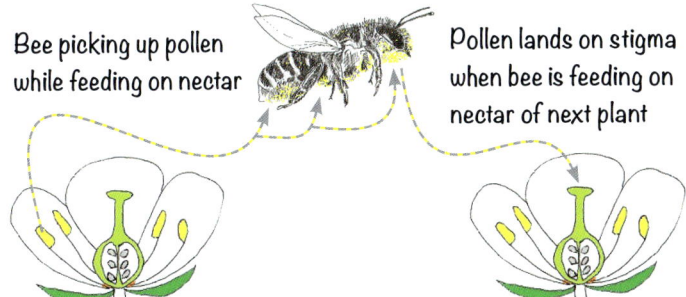

Bee picking up pollen while feeding on nectar

Pollen lands on stigma when bee is feeding on nectar of next plant

How does the pollen travel from one flower to another? Mainly by insects or in some plant species by wind.

- In Britain, bees are the main insect pollinators, less so butterflies, moths and flies. Insect-pollinated flowers are usually showy and coloured to attract the insects, often with scents and a nectar reward.
- Wind-pollinated plants like grasses and trees need to produce a lot of pollen to increase the chance that some pollen grains will land on the target stigma. Their flowers are usually tiny, often green and arranged in catkins as they don't need to attract insects.

Seed Dispersal

Once the ovule has developed into a seed, it has to be dispersed away from the parent plant to give it the best chance to grow. Some plants have ovaries which develop into tasty edible fruits or berries (e.g. blackberries) to attract birds and mammals to carry them farther away. If they eat them the seeds pass through their gut undamaged and land in their dung, ready to germinate and grow. Other seeds are carried away on the wind such as Dandelion parachutes or shaken out like Poppy seeds from their capsule. Some seeds are expelled with an explosive action – Geraniums are an example which use this method. Water plants sometimes have floating seeds which are carried away down the river or lake they grow beside.

Leaf Shapes

Leaf shape also helps to identify a plant. Many leaves are simple in shape such as oval, heart-shaped or long and narrow.

Oval: Chickweed

Long: Iris

Heart shaped: Violet

Round: Pennywort

Others are very divided into lobes – some to the point where one leaf looks like several leaves. These are called compound leaves and the parts are called leaflets. Clover leaves have three leaflets (trefoil) whereas rose leaves have got leaflets in pairs with another leaflet at the end. Leaves can have straight or toothed edges.

Lobed: Ivy

Simple: Daisy

Compound: Rose

Trefoil: Clover

Ferny: Carrot

Toothed: Nettle

Flower Families

Plants are divided into families which group related, usually similar-looking, plant species together. If you can recognise which family an unknown flower belongs to, it becomes much easier to identify it. Some of the most common flower families are listed below.

Rose Family (Rosaceae)
Members of the Rose family include herbs, shrubs or trees. The flowers usually have five petals. The leaves are often compound.

As well as roses, the Rose family includes many edible fruits such as apples, pears, cherries and plums. Strawberries and raspberries also belong to this family.

Cabbage Family (Brassicaceae)
Flowers in the Cabbage family are often white or yellow and have four petals. Because the petals are arranged in a cross, the family is also known as the Crucifer family. Many of our vegetables including cabbage, turnip, broccoli and cauliflower belong to the Cabbage family.

Carrot Family (Apiaceae)

The Carrot family has many small flowers in large flat heads called umbels which give the family its other name of umbellifers. You can remember this name by thinking that the heads look like umbrellas. The flowers are usually white, but some are green or yellow. Many members are used as food or herbs (parsley, dill, fennel), but the family also contains some very poisonous plants (Hemlock, Giant Hogweed).

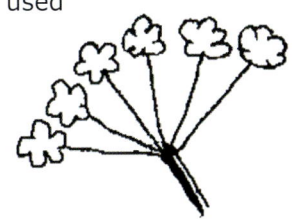

Daisy Family (Asteraceae)

The flowers of the Daisy family are known as composite flowers because what looks like a single flower is actually a group of many tiny flowers. So a daisy 'flower' is in fact many flowers joined together. These flowers can be tubular as in the centre of a Daisy or strap shaped as in the white outer 'petals' of the Daisy.

Pea Family (Fabaceae)

Plants in the Pea family have unusually shaped flowers. The five petals are arranged so that the stamens and stigma are inside a pocket (called the keel) made by two petals, with two side petals (called wings) and a large upright petal (the standard) on top. This arrangement helps trap bees long enough to ensure that the pollen collects on the bee's hairy body and hence is carried to another flower of the same species. The seeds grow inside a pod.

Buttercup Family (Ranunculaceae)

Buttercups and their relatives usually have five-petalled flowers with many stamens. They are often yellow.

Scientific Names

The common names of plants can be misleading as one species of plant may have several common names and different species may have the same name. Using the scientific name solves these problems as every species has a unique scientific name. Scientific names are always in Latin and have two parts. The first refers to the Genus, which is a group of closely related plants, and the second refers to one particular species only. For example, the Wood Anemone has the scientific name *Anemone nemorosa*, where *Anemone* is the Genus containing several Anemone species and *nemorosa* is the single species of Wood Anemone. One main advantage of knowing and using scientific names is that all scientists round the world will recognise what plant you are referring to. Common names, however, can be very different in different countries.

The common and scientific names, including families, of plants mentioned in the text are as detailed in *New Flora of the British Isles* – 4th Ed., Clive Stace, 2019, C&M Floristics.

Woodlands

Woodlands in spring are among our most beautiful sights with carpets of starry white Wood Anemones or the misty blue of Bluebells. These flowers open and set seed quickly. However, once the tree leaves open and cast a shade onto the ground the flowers die back.

In a dense pine forest the floor is often bare all year round, although some plants can grow where trees are spaced well apart, allowing light in.

Bluebell

Hyacinthoides non-scripta
Asparagus family (Asparagaceae)

A Bluebell wood in spring is beautiful to see.

> The bells all hang from the same side of a curved stem. They are a deep blue with a delicate scent and have six petals which curve outwards.

The narrow leaves are long and pointed with a glossy sheen. After flowering, the leaves make food to store in the bulb, from which they grow, for the next year. Be careful not to trample on the leaves as this obviously damages them and, in the end, affects how much food they can make.

Lesser Celandine
Ficaria verna
Buttercup family (Ranunculaceae)

Lesser Celandine, a common spring flower, is a small, low-growing plant. It is not related to Greater Celandine which belongs to a different family.

The starry yellow flowers open in sunlight and close in bad weather. The petals turn white as the flower ages. The number of petals of each flower varies from 5 to 12. Each flower has many stamens.

The leaves are round and often blotched.

WOODLANDS

WOODLANDS

Wild Daffodil
Narcissus pseudonarcissus
Daffodil family (Amaryllidaceae)

Wild Daffodils grow in woods but can also be found in grassland and on cliffs. They are more delicate looking than their garden relatives and flower later in spring. The poet William Wordsworth wrote a famous poem about daffodils. They are also the national flower of Wales.

> Their flowers have pale yellow petals and droop downward. They spread well from seed and carpet the ground.

The leaves are long and narrow.

Dog's Mercury
Mercurialis perennis
Spurge family (Euphorbiaceae)

Dog's Mercury carpets the woodland floor in spring.

> The tiny, green male and female flowers grow on separate plants. The male flowers grow in a spike.

The leaves are oval shaped with toothed edges.

WOODLANDS

Lords-and-Ladies
Arum maculatum
Lords-and-Ladies family (Araceae)

This is one of our most unusual spring flowers; other names are Wild Arum and Cuckoo Pint. The spathe, a specialized leaf, surrounds a fleshy club-shaped structure, called a spadix, typical for this flower family. It can grow up to 50 cm in height.

The tiny flowers are hidden in the swollen base of the spathe. The male and female flowers are separate, and, after pollination by flies, the female flowers develop into a spike of red berries in the autumn. These are **poisonous** as are all parts of the plant.

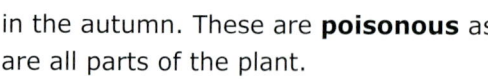

The spathe and the arrow-shaped leaves are often covered in purple spots and blotches.

Primrose
Primula vulgaris
Primrose family (Primulaceae)

(i) The name means First Rose as it flowers early in the year.

Primroses, about 10 cm tall, have pale yellow flowers with a darker centre. The flowers have five heart-shaped petals joined into a tube. The flowers must be cross-pollinated by insects, including moths, to produce seeds. To enable this, Primroses have two different kinds of flowers. One has a long stigma which looks like a pin in the centre of the flower (a pin flower) and the other has a short stigma with long stamens in the centre (a thrum flower – thrums are the loose threads at the edge of woven cloth).

The leaves are long and round at the end, with a crinkly surface.

Ramsons
Allium ursinum
Daffodil family (Amaryllidaceae)

(i) Ramsons often carpets woods and roadsides in spring making a beautiful sight. It is a kind of wild onion as you will realise if you crush the broad leaves. On a warm day you can actually smell Ramsons before you see the flowers. Its other name is Wild Garlic.

The white, star-shaped flowers grow clustered together in heads. They have six petals.

The leaves are large, glossy and oval shaped.

WOODLANDS

Wood Anemone
Anemone nemorosa
Buttercup family (Ranunculaceae)

Wood Anemones, or Windflowers, carpet many woodlands in spring. Because the plants spread slowly, they are thought to show that the wood is very old.

The white starry flowers grow from thin underground stems called rhizomes. Each flowering stem has a single flower. The white 'petals' are actually sepals and can vary in number from five to twelve, with six being the most common. They are often tinged with pink, especially on the outside. The flowers close at night and in bad weather.

At the base of each flower stem are three very divided leaves.

Wood-sorrel
Oxalis acetosella
Wood-sorrel family (Oxalidaceae)

(i) This plant is an indicator of ancient woods, as is the Wood Anemone listed on page 27.

> Wood-sorrel is a small plant with delicate white flowers. The five petals have a network of purple veins. They droop in damp weather.

The leaves have three parts and resemble clover leaves, although this plant is not related to clover.

Red Campion *Silene dioica*
White Campion *Silene latifolia*
Pink family (Caryophyllaceae)

Red Campion grows on grasslands and road verges as well as in woods. It has a long flowering period from May to November and even longer in mild areas. The plants are about 30 to 45 cm tall.

It has a very pretty flower with five deep pink (not red) petals. The male and female flowers grow on separate plants. White Campion is very similar but has white flowers and grows in open spaces.

The oval-shaped leaves and stems are hairy.

WOODLANDS

Stinking Iris
Iris foetidissima
Iris family (Iridaceae)

This is a very interesting plant. It is also called Gladdon.

The flowers, which appear in summer, are pale purple and not very impressive but are followed by beautiful bright orange-red berries in the autumn.

It gets its name from the smell of its long narrow leaves – tear one and smell the torn edge. It smells of roast beef! Rabbits avoid eating the leaves and will starve rather than eat them.

Wood Avens
Geum urbanum
Rose family (Rosaceae)

Wood Avens belongs to the Rose family.

It is quite a tall plant with yellow, five-petalled flowers. The petals are wide apart with spaces between them. The flowers are followed by a ball of hooked fruits which catch on the fur of passing animals and are thus carried away to new areas.

The leaves are compound with the end leaflet being the largest.

WOODLANDS

Snowdrop
Galanthus nivalis
Daffodil family (Amaryllidaceae)

(i) Snowdrops appear early in the year. They are small plants which grow in clumps. Although they are now common in the wild, they were originally brought to Britain as garden plants hundreds of years ago.

Their white, bell-shaped flowers often grow through the snow. The inner petals have green edges.

The leaves are long and very narrow.

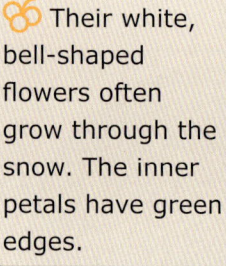

Sweet Violet *Viola odorata*
Common Dog Violet *Viola riviniana*
Violet family (Violaceae)

(i) The purple flowers of the Sweet Violet (on left) are among the earliest to appear, often before January. Their name comes from their sweet scent. In Victorian times street sellers sold posies of Sweet Violets so that people could sniff them to hide the horrible stench on the streets. The blue-violet Dog Violet flowers later in March or April and has no scent.

The flowers are asymmetrical with a spur at the back.

Violets have heart-shaped leaves. Those of Sweet Violets are hairy; Dog Violets' leaves are hairless.

Butcher's Broom
Ruscus aculeatus
Asparagus family (Asparagaceae)

This is a small, prickly shrub. Butchers used to scrub their chopping blocks with bunches of them.

If you look closely you will see a single, tiny, cream flower underneath the centre of each 'leaf'. It has six petals. Male and female flowers grow on separate bushes. In autumn the female flowers each develop into a large, bright red berry which hangs under the 'leaf'.

The glossy, lance-shaped, green structures that look like 'leaves' are actually flattened stems.

Enchanter's Nightshade
Circaea lutetiana
Willowherb family (Onagraceae)

The enchanter of the name is Circe, an enchantress in Greek mythology.

The white flowers are tiny with two petals which are so divided that they look like four. They grow in spikes above the leaves.

The oval leaves grow in pairs.

Heaths and Moors

Heaths, in the south of Britain, and moors in the north, often in upland areas, have a typical cover of heather and few trees. They provide perfect habitats for many mammals and ground-nesting birds.

Heaths tend to be dryer, whereas moors are damper, but both have nutrient-poor soil allowing only well-adapted plants to grow.

Broom

Cytisus scoparius
Pea family (Fabaceae)

HEATHS AND MOORS

(i) Broom is a small ever-green shrub with flowers which are very similar to Gorse (page 39) and also flower in spring.

🌼 The flowers are bright yellow. They look like those of peas, and indeed the plant belongs to the Pea family. The seed pods turn black when ripe.

🌱 The three-parted leaves are tiny. The ridged stems are not prickly, as they are in Gorse.

Gorse
Ulex europaeus
Pea family (Fabaceae)

An old saying states that 'Kissing is out of fashion when the gorse is not in bloom'. However, you will find some Gorse in bloom all year round, although the main flowering time is in spring. Then the heaths are yellow with the flowers on the Gorse bushes.

These flowers are like miniature pea flowers and so the plant belongs to the Pea family, as Broom does (page 38). The pods of seeds are like miniature hairy pea pods. They dry out and then explode with a loud pop to scatter the seeds. The flowers have a strong scent of coconut.

Gorse doesn't have leaves as they have evolved into thorns.

HEATHS AND MOORS

Bilberry
Vaccinium myrtillus
Heather family (Ericaceae)

Bilberry or Blaeberry grows as small bushes on moors. It is related to Heather.

It has bell-shaped flowers, similar to heather, although they are larger and pale pink. They are followed in autumn by the Blaeberries which are dark blue, almost black, with a grey bloom, and resemble small blueberries.

The leathery leaves are small, oval and a glossy green.

Common Cottongrass
Eriophorum angustifolium
Sedge family (Cyperaceae)

This is actually a sedge, not a grass. Sedges have solid stems, which are often triangular in cross-section, and grow in wet areas, whereas grasses have hollow stems in cross-section and tend to grow in drier areas. Cottongrass grows in the wetter areas of moorland, also marshes, so be very careful where you walk if you want a close look at it.

It has small green flowers which turn into the characteristic seed heads after fertilisation. They are fluffy and white, and stand out above the moor.

Leaves are dark green and narrow.

HEATHS AND MOORS

HEATHS AND MOORS

Dodder
Cuscuta epithymum
Bindweed family (Convolvulaceae)

(i) In late summer you may see Gorse and Heather covered in masses of thin red stems. This is Dodder. As it has no green pigment, it cannot make its own food from sunlight and grows as a parasite on another plant, tapping into its sap to get its food.

It has clusters of tiny, pink flowers. It is related to bindweed.

The leaves are reduced to tiny scales. Because the stems are so thin and weak, they have given us the word 'doddery', meaning frail and shaky.

Harebell
Campanula rotundifolia
Bellflower family (Campanulaceae)

(i) This is one of the bellflowers. In Scotland it is called a Bluebell.

🍂 The lilac-blue flowers are bell shaped and quite large for the size of the plant.

🌱 It is a very delicate plant with thin stems and narrow leaves, although the leaves at the base of the stem are round.

HEATHS AND MOORS

HEATHS AND MOORS

Milkwort
Polygala vulgaris
Milkwort family (Polygalaceae)

(i) Milkwort is a tiny plant of dry heaths.

It is usually deep blue, but pink or white flowers are sometimes seen.

The coloured 'petals' are actually coloured leaves which enclose the tiny flower inside. There are normal green leaves, narrow and pointed, further down the stem.

Sheep's-bit
Jasione montana
Bellflower family (Campanulaceae)

(i) Sheep's-bit is related to the bellflowers. It grows also in coastal sites.

🌼 It has small, blue, button-like flowers growing on long stems – another name for it is Bachelor's Buttons. Each flower is actually a group of many tiny flowers which open from the outside in.

🌱 The leaves are long and narrow, growing in a clump.

HEATHS AND MOORS

Heather *Calluna vulgaris*
Bell Heather *Erica cinerea*
Heather family (Ericaceae)

(i) There are several kinds of heather, mostly with purple or pink flowers, tiny leaves and woody stems.

Heather (left), or Ling, has spikes of tiny lilac flowers. Occasionally you might find a plant of Ling with white flowers – the lucky white Heather. Bell Heather (right) has larger, deep purple, bell-shaped flowers.

The green leaves are scale-like. Wild Grouse feed on the young shoots.

HEATHS AND MOORS

Tormentil
Potentilla erecta
Rose family (Rosaceae)

(i) The name originates from its former use to relieve pain (or torment). It often creeps along the ground.

> The yellow flowers have four petals.

The leaves are compound with five toothed leaflets looking like the fingers of a hand.

HEATHS AND MOORS

Walls

Walls and older pavements provide habitats for plants that can survive with little water and soil and must withstand the baking heat of the stones on hot summer days. Many wall plants have succulent leaves to store water. Also, their seeds need to find crevices and cracks between the stones where it is cool and dark so that they can germinate safely. As well as flowering plants, you will also find ferns here.

Navelwort
Umbilicus rupestris
Stonecrop family (Crassulaceae)

(i) This plant is more common in the west of Britain. Another name for it is Pennywort.

In late spring and summer a spike of creamy-white tubular flowers appears. This can grow up to 30 cm tall.

With its round fleshy leaves, it is easy to see where this plant gets its name from.

Ivy-leaved Toadflax
Cymbalaria muralis
Speedwell family (Veronicaceae)

You can find this trailing plant on many old walls, even pathways.

If you look closely at the flowers of Ivy-leaved Toadflax you will see that they are like miniature versions of the Snapdragon common in gardens. These are very pretty with their purple and lemon colouring. When the seeds are ripe, the flowering stems grow into a crack in the wall so that the seeds are dispersed in just the right place for them to germinate and grow next year.

As the name suggests, the leaves are like miniature Ivy leaves.

WALLS

Pellitory-of-the-wall
Parietaria judaica
Nettle family (Urticaceae)

(ⓘ) This plant spreads out over the wall. It also grows on roadside verges and here it can grow much larger with the increased nutrients of the deeper soil. It is related to nettles and is also the larval foodplant for the Red Admiral butterfly.

🌼 Its reddish flowers are tiny and grow in clusters at the end of the stems.

🌱 It has oval leaves and reddish stems. The leaves feel bristly as they are covered in tiny hairs.

English Stonecrop *Sedum anglicum*
Biting Stonecrop *Sedum acre*
Stonecrop family (Crassulaceae)

(i) There are several types of stonecrop, or Sedum species. The Sedum that is used to cover eco-friendly roofs is related to stonecrops.

The flowers are like little stars. These are white in the English Stonecrop and yellow in Biting Stonecrop.

All types have small, thick, succulent leaves which help retain water.

WALLS

Mexican Fleabane
Erigeron karvinskianus
Daisy family (Asteraceae)

Originally a garden plant from Mexico but it escaped and is now widespread over much of the UK, although it hasn't reached many of the regions of Scotland yet.

It has delicate, white, daisy-like flowers. Some flowers may be pink.

The leaves are long and narrow.

Red Valerian
Centranthus ruber
Valerian family (Valerianaceae)

(i) Originally a garden plant from the Mediterranean which escaped many years ago and is now common in England and Wales, although rare in Scotland.

Bees and other insects visit the clusters of tiny deep pink flowers. These have five petals with a spur at the back. You may find a white-flowered plant.

The oval leaves are grey-green.

Dunes and Seashore

Seashore plants are specialised to survive strong winds and salt spray. To prevent water loss from the leaves, these plants have adapted to this environment by developing leaves that are either small or thick and waxy. Very few plants can cope with the shifting sand on sandy beaches, usually above the high tide mark, but may not survive long. Further back, sand dunes may develop. Some plants can grow on shingle (stony) beaches but, again, above the high tide mark.

Marram
Ammophila arenaria
Grass family (Poaceae)

(i) Marram grass is essential for the formation of sand dunes as its long roots hold the sand grains together and other plants can then start to colonise the dunes.

> Cream to pale yellow flowers are displayed on long spikes.

Its leaves are grey due to a thick, waxy protective layer which prevents water loss. If you look closely at a leaf you will see that it is rolled into a tube so that the underside of the leaf is completely enclosed. This reduces water evaporation from the tiny pores on the underside of the leaf.

Sea Bindweed
Calystegia soldanella
Bindweed family (Convolvulaceae)

Sea Bindweed grows close to the ground to avoid the seashore winds. Unlike its relatives, Hedge and Field Bindweed (page 101), its roots do not grow deep enough for it to become a problem for gardeners.

The trumpet-shaped flowers are very pretty, pink with five white stripes.

Its fleshy leaves help it to store moisture. They are kidney-shaped.

Sea Campion
Silene uniflora
Pink family (Caryophyllaceae)

(i) This plant is often found growing on cliffs. Despite its name, Sea Campion can also grow quite a long way from the coast. The whole plant is small to avoid the sea winds, and the stems grow in a tight cushion to help reduce water loss.

> It has white flowers, with a puffed-up calyx, which grow singly on stems.

The leaves are grey-green and fleshy.

Sea-holly
Eryngium maritimum
Carrot family (Apiaceae)

The prickly leaves of this plant give it its name, but it is not related to Holly.

Even though the flowers resemble those of thistles, in fact it is an umbellifer and belongs to the same family as Wild Carrot. It has many tiny blue flowers that are tightly packed on a cone-like structure.

The leaves have a thick, waxy coating to prevent moisture loss and this is why they are blue-green in colour.

DUNES AND SEASHORE

Thrift
Armeria maritima
Thrift family (Plumbaginaceae)

(i) In May, cliff ledges and other areas close to the sea are often pink with the flowers of Thrift. It is also called Sea Pink.

The pink flower heads, each containing many tiny flowers, grow singly on long stems.

The plant produces cushions of long, narrow leaves.

Sea-lavender
Limonium species
Thrift family (Plumbaginaceae)

Sea-lavender is not related to the garden Lavender and does not have a smell. There are several very similar species growing in Britain.

The flowers are bluish-purple, including the calyx. After the petals fall the calyx remains for a long time.

The leaves are long and oval, growing in a rosette.

DUNES AND SEASHORE

Marshes, Lakes and Rivers

Be careful when you look for plants in these habitats as marshes can be treacherous and you may get wet feet or worse. Many plants like to grow in damp areas, even in ponds and rivers. In wet areas of marshes you can find sundews (see inset) that have sticky leaves to trap insects which they digest to get extra nutrients. These are known as carnivorous plants.

Lady's Smock
Cardamine pratensis
Cabbage family (Brassicaceae)

(i) Lady's Smock grows in damp meadows, pond margins and along streams. The 'Lady' in the name is the Virgin Mary, mother of Jesus. Many wild flowers have Lady in their name. Another name for this plant is Cuckooflower because it flowers in spring around the time that the cuckoo arrives.

Its pink flowers have four petals showing that it belongs to the Cabbage family.

The compound leaves are very divided.

Ragged-Robin
Silene flos-cuculi
Pink family (Caryophyllaceae)

Ragged-Robin likes to grow in wet meadows and marshes. It is related to Campions and Catchflies. It flowers in late spring.

The ragged pink petals of the flower give it its name. Each flower has five petals but they are so divided and split that you would think there are many more.

It has lance-shaped leaves.

MARSHES, LAKES AND RIVERS

Marsh-marigold
Caltha palustris
Buttercup family (Ranunculaceae)

(ⓘ) This beautiful plant grows in the marshy ground at the edge of lakes and rivers, sometimes even in the water. It belongs to the Buttercup family. Another name for it is Kingcup.

> Its bright yellow flowers look like large Buttercups.

The leaves are large, round and glossy.

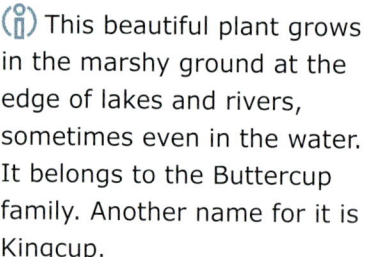

Bulrush
Typha latifolia
Bulrush family (Typhaceae)

The old name for this plant is Reedmace. It grows at the edges of ponds, streams and rivers.

The flower stems can be up to 2 metres tall. At the end of the stem is a brown, furry swelling which is actually made of hundreds of female flowers. The male flowers are above these. The ripe seeds are carried away on fluffy parachutes by the wind.

The leaves are long and pointed.

MARSHES, LAKES AND RIVERS

Meadowsweet
Filipendula ulmaria
Rose family (Rosaceae)

Meadowsweet grows in damp meadows and along rivers. It belongs to the Rose family. Hundreds of years ago it was used as a strewing herb on the floors of houses to keep them smelling sweet.

The spikes of the frothy cream flowers have a strong, sweet scent.

It has dark green, divided compound leaves.

Purple-loosestrife
Lythrum salicaria
Purple-loosestrife family (Lythraceae)

(i) Purple-loosestrife likes to grow at the edge of lakes and rivers. It is a tall, hairy plant, up to 2 metres tall.

The purple flowers grow along tall spikes in whorls on the stem, each with six petals and twelve stamens.

The leaves are unstalked and narrow.

MARSHES, LAKES AND RIVERS

White Water-lily *Nymphaea alba*
Yellow Water-lily *Nuphar lutea*
Water-lily family (Nymphaeaceae)

In Britain we have two common species – the White and the Yellow Water-lily.

The White Water-lily has very large, open, floating flowers with many petals and stamens. The Yellow Water-lily has smaller flowers which are more cup shaped. They are related to the tropical Lotus flower.

Water-lilies have large, round, floating leaves.

Water Mint
Mentha aquatica
Dead-nettle family (Lamiaceae)

There are many wild mints. Water Mint is common beside ponds and streams.

> The pink flowers grow in round clusters at the top of the stem in summer. Bumblebees and honey bees visit them to feed on nectar.

The leaves look like Garden Mint and have a minty smell when crushed.

MARSHES, LAKES AND RIVERS

Yellow Iris
Iris pseudacorus
Iris family (Iridaceae)

(i) This is a tall plant with yellow flowers. Another name for Yellow Iris is Yellow Flag which has nothing to do with the flags we fly but is from an old word for sword and refers to the leaves.

The yellow flowers have an unusual shape and are thought to be the origin of the fleur de lis emblem of France.

The leaves are long and sword shaped.

Water Avens
Geum rivale
Rose family (Rosaceae)

Water Avens is very closely related to Wood Avens (page 31) and sometimes crosses with it to produce hybrid plants with flowers intermediate between the two parents.

The flowers are drooping, with salmon-pink petals and purple sepals.

The leaves are compound and toothed.

Gardens and Parks

Many of the weeds in our gardens and parks are beautiful if you look closely. Dandelions would be highly prized by gardeners if they were rare and difficult to grow. Weeds have several survival strategies. Some produce many seeds to rapidly colonise bare spaces. Those which grow in lawns are usually low growing so that they survive regular mowing. They often have a flat rosette of leaves. Many flower almost all year round; the seasons given here are only the main flowering times.

Daisy
Bellis perennis
Daisy family (Asteraceae)

(i) The name comes from 'Day's Eye'.

Although a Daisy flower looks like a single flower, it is actually made up of many tiny ones. Each white 'petal' and each yellow bump in the centre is a separate flower. You can play the game of 'He loves me, he loves me not' by pulling off a few white 'petals' at a time.

The leaves are small and rounded.

Dandelion
Taraxacum officinale
Daisy family (Asteraceae)

This is another member of the Daisy family. The name comes from the French Dent de lion, meaning lion's tooth, describing the toothed edges of the leaves.

The shaggy, yellow flowers are followed by dandelion clocks where each seed has a little parachute to carry it away on the wind. When you break the flower stem a milky sap oozes out.

They are very difficult to remove from lawns as their leaves grow in flat rosettes which escape the lawnmower. If you try to pull one up you will find it has a long root and it is easy to leave some of this root in the ground. A new Dandelion will grow from any root fragment left behind.

GARDENS AND PARKS

Chickweed
Stellaria media
Pink family (Caryophyllaceae)

Chickweed spreads over the ground or through the grass on lawns to form a mat. Rabbits enjoy eating its juicy leaves and stems.

It has tiny, white, five-petalled flowers which are so divided that they look like ten petals.

Its broad, oval leaves grow in pairs on the stem.

White Clover *Trifolium repens*
Red Clover *Trifolium pratense*
Pea family (Fabaceae)

There are many kinds of clover. White and Red Clover are the ones most commonly found as weeds in lawns.

The flowers are grouped into round flower heads and have a sweet scent. They produce large quantities of nectar, which bees and butterflies feed on using their long tongues to reach the nectar at the bottom of the flower tubes.

All clovers have the familiar leaves in three parts. This shape is called a trefoil and is the symbol used by Rainbows, Brownies and Guides. It is also similar to the shamrock – Ireland's national plant.

Groundsel
Senecio vulgaris
Daisy family (Asteraceae)

Groundsel belongs to the same flower family as daisies and dandelions.

It has small yellow flower heads which are followed by fluffy seeds. These are carried by the wind and spread to new areas of bare ground.

The leaves are divided into lobes. Rabbits enjoy a little Groundsel as a treat.

Scarlet Pimpernel
Lysimachia arvensis
Primrose family (Primulaceae)

This low-growing plant scrambles over waste ground and across lawns.

Scarlet Pimpernel is one of the very few red British flowers, although you can also find it with white or blue flowers. The five-petalled flowers close up in bad weather which explains the alternative name of Poor Man's Weatherglass. The seed capsule is like a little green ball which splits in half when ripe to allow the seeds to disperse.

The leaves are oval and pointed with black dots on the underside.

Shepherd's-purse
Capsella bursa-pastoris
Cabbage family (Brassicaceae)

(i) You find them in flower beds and borders, and along paths.

The name comes from the heart-shaped seed capsules which follow the tiny white flowers. They are supposed to resemble the purses shepherds wore around their waist. The flowers have four petals and so Shepherd's-purse belongs to the Cabbage family.

The leaves grow in a rosette near the ground as well as up the stem.

Fox-and-cubs
Pilosella aurantiaca
Daisy family (Asteraceae)

Originally a garden plant but it escaped and grows in several habitats including gardens and roadsides.

The flowers are orange-red in a cluster.

It has a rosette of leaves at ground level as well as leaves on the hairy stems.

GARDENS AND PARKS

Hedgerows and Roadsides

Many wild flowers grow on roadside verges and along hedgerows. In fact, the older the hedge the more different kind of trees and shrubs you will find; a hedge may be all that is left of an old wood. Hedges not only provide shelter and food for many wildlife species but are also important connections between woods allowing animals to travel safely from one wood to another.

Blackthorn
Prunus spinosa
Rose family (Rosaceae)

Blackthorn is a small thorny shrub with dark stems. The flowers of the Blackthorn are among the first to appear in spring before its leaves appear.

These white, five-petalled flowers develop into fruits called sloes which look like tiny plums, although they are far too bitter for us to eat. In fact, the Blackthorn is thought to be one of the ancestors of the plum.

The leaves are oval and toothed. Be wary of the thorns.

Colt's-foot
Tussilago farfara
Daisy family (Asteraceae)

Colt's-foot often grows on bare ground.

The yellow flowers look like small Dandelions and they belong to the same family. The flowers turn orange as they age, and the seed heads look like miniature dandelion clocks.

Colt's-foot gets its name from the hoof-shaped leaves which appear after the flowers in spring. These leaves have downy undersides.

HEDGEROWS AND ROADSIDES

Cowslip
Primula veris
Primrose family (Primulaceae)

(i) Cowslips are related to Primroses, shown on page 25. As well as growing on roadsides, you will also find them in deciduous woodland.

❀ The yellow flowers grow in a drooping group at the end of a tall stem. They are smaller and more cupped than Primrose flowers.

🌿 The rosette of leaves is very similar to that of a Primrose.

Hawthorn
Crataegus monogyna
Rose family (Rosaceae)

Hawthorn is a shrub or small tree often found in hedgerows. It is also known as the May-tree.

It belongs to the Rose family as shown by its five-petalled flowers which open in spring. These are usually white, although they can occasionally be pink. They have a sickly sweet scent. In autumn they are followed by red berries called haws, which are inedible to us but birds relish them.

The leaves are lobed.

HEDGEROWS AND ROADSIDES

Greater Stitchwort *Stellaria holostea*
Lesser Stichwort *Stellaria graminea*
Pink family (Caryophyllaceae)

You can find both the Greater and the Lesser Stitchwort along hedges and roadsides in large patches. Greater Stitchwort flowers are 2 to 3 cm across with the flowers of the Lesser Stitchwort being half that, up to 1.5 cm.

> Both Stitchwort species have delicate white flowers with five petals that are almost divided into two. This makes them look like stars. The seed pod pops open when ripe to fire the seeds in all directions. You can make it pop by touching it.

The leaves are long and narrow on brittle stems.

Cow Parsley
Anthriscus sylvestris
Carrot family (Apiaceae)

The frothy white flowers of Cow Parsley turn the roadsides white in May. It can grow up to the height of an adult person.

Its flat heads of many tiny flowers show that it belongs to the Umbellifer or Carrot family as do Wild Carrot and Hogweed.

It is easily recognised by its ferny leaves.

HEDGEROWS AND ROADSIDES

Ramping-fumitory
Fumaria muralis
Poppy family (Papaveraceae)

Ramping-fumitory straggles up the hedgerows in spring and summer. It is similar to the more widespread Common Fumitory (*F. officinalis*).

It has spikes of purple-pink flowers. These are tubular. Each develops into a round fruit like a tiny bead.

The leaves are greyish-green and very divided, looking like fern leaves.

Jack-by-the-hedge
Alliaria petiolata
Cabbage family (Brassicaceae)

It is also known as Garlic Mustard or Hedge Garlic because the shiny leaves smell of garlic when crushed. This plant belongs to the Cabbage family. It is quite a tall plant, up to 60 cm tall.

It has clusters of white flowers at the top of each stem. It flowers in spring and early summer.

The leaves are broad, heart-shaped and toothed.

Blackberry
Rubus fruticosus
Rose family (Rosaceae)

(i) Also known as Bramble.

🐝 Blackberry flowers are usually white but can also be pink. They have five petals and many stamens and belong to the Rose family. The glossy, purple-black fruits are edible and used in puddings and to make jam. Just be careful of the thorns when you're picking them!

🌱 The leaves usually have five leaflets and often have white wriggly lines where leaf miner caterpillars have made their tunnels.

Comfrey
Symphytum officinale
Borage family (Boraginaceae)

Comfrey is a tall, very hairy plant. Bumblebees visit it to search for nectar.

Groups of tubular flowers hang down near the top of the plant. They are five-petalled and usually purple but can also be creamy white.

It has large, wide, oval leaves.

HEDGEROWS AND ROADSIDES

Broad-leaved Dock
Rumex obtusifolius
Knotweed family (Polygonaceae)

(i) There are many different kinds of dock. Broad-leaved Dock with large leaves is the one traditionally used to rub on nettle stings. There is no evidence that they are particularly effective, but the large leaves do cool the stung area and are not poisonous, so they are worth a try.

The flowers grow in a branched spike above the leaves. They are green and followed by brown seeds.

Leaves are broad and oval-shaped with a tip at the end. The sides are smooth and slightly wavy.

Elder
Sambucus nigra
Moschatel family (Adoxaceae)

This is a small tree. A mature one can be up to 15 metres tall.

The heads of creamy-white, scented flowers in early summer are followed by purple-black berries. Birds feast on them, and the berries turn their droppings purple!

It has compound leaves. The stems are hollow, filled with a spongy pith. Children used to push out the pith to make whistles from the stems.

HEDGEROWS AND ROADSIDES

Cleavers
Galium aparine
Bedstraw family (Rubiaceae)

Cleavers, also called Goosegrass, is a relative of Lady's Bedstraw.

It has tiny, green, four-petalled flowers followed by round, green seeds covered in hooks.

Cleavers leaves and the four-sided stems are covered in tiny hooks which stick to the fur of passing animals or the clothes of people. This explains the other name of Sticky Willie. Children love to play tricks on their friends by sticking pieces to their backs and seeing how long it takes them to notice. You can see these tiny hooks on the edges of the leaves and stems in the photo.

Hedge Bindweed *Calystegia sepium*
Field Bindweed *Convolvulus arvensis*
Bindweed family (Convolvulaceae)

Hedge Bindweed scrambles over hedges, coiling in a clockwise direction. However, Field Bindweed tends to grow along the ground, although it will climb up fence posts. Farmers find it a pest as its roots grow very deep and it is very difficult to dig up.

The flowers of Hedge Bindweed are like large white trumpets and those of Field Bindweed are smaller with pink trumpets.

The leaves of both are arrow shaped.

Herb-Robert
Geranium robertianum
Crane's-bill family (Geraniaceae)

(i) Herb-Robert is a Geranium. Wild Geraniums are often called Stork's-bills or Crane's-bills because of their long-pointed fruits which resemble birds' beaks.

It has purple five-petalled flowers.

The leaves are very divided. The leaves and stems of Herb-Robert are often red. They have an unpleasant smell.

Hogweed
Heracleum sphondylium
Carrot family (Apiaceae)

Hogweed gets its name because it used to be fed to pigs. It is a tall plant, about a metre high. The large flower heads are often visited by Red Soldier beetles.

The white flowers have five petals, each having a deep notch so that you might think there were ten petals. The outer petals are larger than the inner ones. Sometimes the flowers are pink.

The hairy leaves are large and divided. The stem is hollow and contains an irritating sap.

HEDGEROWS AND ROADSIDES

Honeysuckle
Lonicera periclymenum
Honeysuckle family (Caprifoliaceae)

Honeysuckle is a climbing plant.

It has clusters of long trumpet-shaped flowers. These are cream with a pink tinge. They have a beautiful scent which is strongest at night to attract the night-flying moths which drink nectar with their long tongues and in so doing pollinate it. The red berries are **poisonous**.

The oval leaves grow in pairs.

Lady's Bedstraw *Galium verum*
Hedge Bedstraw *Galium album*
Bedstraw family (Rubiaceae)

Lady's Bedstraw is a low-growing, sprawling plant. The dried plant was used to stuff mattresses hundreds of years ago.

It has tiny, yellow flowers with four petals. The flowers grow in clusters and so from a distance the plant looks like a froth of yellow. Hedge Bedstraw is very similar but has white flowers.

The dark green leaves are in whorls.

HEDGEROWS AND ROADSIDES

Nettle
Urtica dioica
Nettle family (Urticaceae)

(i) Nettles are important food plants for the caterpillars of several butterflies, including the beautiful Small Tortoiseshell.

The tiny pink or yellow flowers grow in droopy spikes above the leaves.

The stems and leaves of nettles are covered in stinging hairs, therefore also called Stinging Nettles. When you brush against the hairs they penetrate your skin and inject a poison which causes the burning sensation. However, if you grasp the nettle firmly you break the hairs off so that the point can't go through your skin and you don't get stung. The saying 'grasp the nettle' means that if you tackle a problem head on it will be easier.

Lesser Periwinkle
Vinca minor
Periwinkle family (Apocynaceae)

(i) Periwinkle is a ground-covering plant.

Its flowers have five petals. They are very blue and have given their name to a shade of blue.

The leaves are shiny and oval in shape and grow in pairs on stems which scramble through the hedges and undergrowth.

HEDGEROWS AND ROADSIDES

Red Dead-nettle *Lamium purpureum*
White Dead-nettle *Lamium album*
Dead-nettle family (Lamiaceae)

(i) Dead-nettles are so named because they do not sting. They are not closely related to Stinging Nettles even though their leaves look similar. There are several species of Dead-nettle with different coloured flowers.

White Dead-nettle has large white hooded flowers. Red Dead-nettle is a smaller plant with smaller, deep-pink flowers, yet they have the same hooded shape.

They have green, nettle-like leaves.

Rowan
Sorbus aucuparia
Rose family (Rosaceae)

Rowan is a small tree which can grow up to 15 metres tall. A good crop of the red Rowan berries was once thought to indicate that the winter was going to be very cold, thereby providing food for the birds. However, a lot of berries simply means that the weather was good in the preceding spring and summer.

> The plant has large, flat heads, each containing hundreds of creamy-white flowers. These develop into bright red berries which the birds enjoy.

It has compound leaves.

HEDGEROWS AND ROADSIDES

Trailing St John's-wort *Hypericum humifusum*
Perforate St John's-wort *Hypericum perforatum*
St John's-wort family (Hypericaceae)

There are several species of St John's-wort. The photograph on the left shows Trailing St John's-wort growing in a lawn.

All have yellow, five-petalled flowers with many stamens.

The leaves are oval. Several species, like Perforate St John's Wort (right photo), have clear spots which you can see if you hold a leaf up to the light.

Toadflax
Linaria vulgaris
Speedwell family (Veronicaceae)

This is a relative of the Garden Snapdragon. Toadflax usually grows to 30 cm tall but can be much taller.

It has a spike of pale yellow flowers which are very unusual in shape, supposedly resembling a toad's mouth, with a long spur at the back. There is also a purple-flowered species.

The leaves are long and narrow.

HEDGEROWS AND ROADSIDES

Rosebay Willowherb
Chamaenerion angustifolium
Willowherb family (Onagraceae)

It likes to grow on disturbed ground like wasteland and burned areas. This may explain its other name of Fireweed, although the tall flower spikes with pink flowers also look like flames. It often grows in dense stands on roadsides like miniature forests.

The beautiful pink flowers have four petals. Its fluffy seeds are carried on the wind, allowing it to spread rapidly on bare ground. One plant can produce up to 80,000 seeds!

The leaves are long and narrow.

White Bryony
Bryonia dioica
White Bryony family (Cucurbitaceae)

White Bryony scrambles over hedgerows holding its straggly stems in place with coiling tendrils. It is related to cucumbers.

The five-petalled flowers are greenish-white with green veins. The male and female flowers are separate but on the same plant; the female flowers are followed by red berries. These are **poisonous**.

The leaves have five lobes and resemble large Ivy leaves.

Wild Carrot
Daucus carota
Carrot family (Apiaceae)

(i) Wild Carrot is common, especially near the coast.

The head of white flowers often has a red or purple flower in the centre. This may be to signal approaching insects that an insect is already there and so it is safe to land. When the flowers have been pollinated the head of flowers curves inward and looks like a miniature bird's nest.

It has ferny leaves which smell of carrot when crushed.

Traveller's-joy
Clematis vitalba
Buttercup family (Ranunculaceae)

(i) Traveller's-joy, or Wild Clematis, scrambles over walls and fences. It is related to Buttercups.

Although Clematis varieties grown for gardens often have large, showy flowers, Wild Clematis has small, white flowers. Each flower produces many seeds, each with a long feathery plume. These white, fluffy seed heads give the plant its other name of Old Man's Beard. They stay on the plant over winter when the leaves have died, and you will often spot them when travelling by road or train.

The leaves are compound and divided into oval leaflets.

HEDGEROWS AND ROADSIDES

Dog-rose
Rosa canina
Rose family (Rosaceae)

Dog-roses scramble through hedgerows, their weak thorny stems using the hedge shrubs for support. Another name is Briar Rose. Roses are the national plant of England and were the symbol of many Royal houses, including the Tudor kings and queens.

They can have pink or white flowers with five heart-shaped petals and many yellow stamens. After flowering the seed pods develop into rose hips. These are bright red to attract birds which eat them and so disperse the seeds. They are very rich in vitamin C and in the past were made into rose hip syrup.

The leaves are compound and divided into toothed leaflets.

HEDGEROWS AND ROADSIDES

Wild Strawberry
Fragaria vesca
Rose family (Rosaceae)

(ⓘ) This much-loved plant is a member of the Rose family.

🌼 The white flowers have five petals and five sepals and are followed by tiny strawberries which taste very sweet.

🌱 The toothed leaves have three leaflets.

HEDGEROWS AND ROADSIDES

Bittersweet
Solanum dulcamara
Nightshade family (Solanaceae)

ⓘ Also known as Woody Nightshade, Bittersweet belongs to the Nightshade family, and like many members of that family it is **poisonous**. It is a straggly plant, using other plants to support it. It flowers in late summer.

🌼 The flowers have five purple petals arranged like a star and a cone of yellow stamens in the centre. The berries which follow are green, ripening to red.

🌱 The leaves are pointed ovals, often with two little leaflets at the base.

Mallow
Malva sylvestris
Mallow family (Malvaceae)

This Mallow is quite common and can grow up to 1.5 metres tall.

It has pink-purple, five-petalled flowers with heart-shaped petals. The stigma is large and sticks up from the centre of the flower. The seeds are a ring of little nutlets arranged like wedges of a circular cheese.

The leaves have five lobes and are soft and hairy.

HEDGEROWS AND ROADSIDES

Smooth Sowthistle
Sonchus oleraceus
Daisy family (Asteraceae)

Smooth Sowthistle is a tall plant, growing up to 1 metre high. It is related to Dandelions and Daisies.

The flowers are yellow, but smaller and less open than Dandelions.

Whilst the leaves are heavily toothed, these are soft and not prickly like a true thistle.

Ivy
Hedera helix
Ivy family (Araliaceae)

HEDGEROWS AND ROADSIDES

Ivy climbs up trees and walls. It doesn't harm them, but it may make trees top-heavy and more likely to fall down in high winds.

This is one of the last plants to flower in the year. Its round clusters of green flowers appear in autumn and the nectar is much appreciated by late-flying insects, including bees and butterflies.

The black berries which follow are eaten by birds.

Leaves near the ground are five-pointed but higher up they change shape to simple ovals; the Ivy is then called Tree Ivy.

121

Fields

Fields where farmers grow crops have far fewer wild flowers now than formerly, due to modern farming methods. However, you may still see these flowers along the field margins. Some farmers will grow wild flowers here and these may include rare plants like Corn Cockle and Cornflower. These wild flowers attract many insects which will also pollinate the crop nearby.

FIELDS

Goosefoot
Chenopodium album
Amaranth family (Chenopodiaceae)

(ⓘ) The name Goosefoot relates to the diamond shape of the leaves which resemble a goose's webbed foot. It is also called Fat-hen.

🌼 The flowers grow in a spike above the leaves and are very small and green.

🌿 The diamond-shaped leaves are coated with a wax and therefore don't get wet. Underneath they have a white coat.

Corn Marigold
Glebionis segetum
Daisy family (Asteraceae)

(i) Corn Marigold is less common now than it used to be, but you might still see it around the edges of arable fields in summer. It grows about 15 to 20 cm tall.

> The beautiful flower looks like a large yellow Daisy.

The leaves are lobed.

FIELDS

Oxeye Daisy
Leucanthemum vulgare
Daisy family (Asteraceae)

This is a large plant in the Daisy family, growing up to 60 cm high.

Its flowers are like Daisies with white 'petals' and yellow centres but are much larger, up to 4 cm across.

It has dark green, lobed leaves.

Pineappleweed
Matricaria discoidea
Daisy family (Asteraceae)

This weed of fields and tracks is a member of the Daisy family, although at first glance you may not realise that.

On closer inspection you will see that the green, dome-shaped flowers are like the centre of a Daisy without the outer 'petals'. If you crush them you will find that they have a strong sweet scent, although you will need a good imagination to recognise it as that of a pineapple.

It has very divided leaves.

Ribwort Plantain
Plantago lanceolata
Plantain family (Plantaginaceae)

There are several species of plantain occurring in the UK. One of them is Ribwort Plantain, as shown here.

The brown flower heads grow on long stems which are often grooved and square. Each flower head is made up of many flowers packed together. If you look closely you will see a ring of stamens hanging out of each flower head. Children used to play a game trying to knock the flower head off their rival's stems – a bit like a game of conkers.

Ribwort Plantain has a rosette of long, oval leaves with several veins running along their length.

Corn Poppy
Papaver rhoeas
Poppy family (Papaveraceae)

Poppies are one of the few red British wild flowers, flowering in fields and waste places in summer.

The beautiful flowers have four crinkly petals which only last a day or so before falling off. The red petals often have a black base. Two hairy green sepals protect the flower bud but fall off as the flower opens. The stamens are black. The ripe seed pod develops holes near the top so that when the wind blows the tiny black seeds are shaken out like pepper from a pepper pot.

The stems and lobed leaves are hairy.

FIELDS

Scentless Mayweed
Tripleurospermum inodorum
Daisy family (Asteraceae)

Scentless Mayweed grows in arable fields, quite close to the ground to a height of around 10–15 cm.

It has white, unscented flowers like large Daisies.

The leaves are ferny.

Ragwort
Jacobaea vulgaris
Daisy family (Asteraceae)

Ragwort is a very **poisonous** plant, yet insects visit the flowers for their nectar. The only animal which can safely eat the leaves is the caterpillar of the Cinnabar Moth which absorbs the poison and becomes poisonous itself. It warns predators of this with its bright orange and black stripes.

It is a tall plant which has flat clusters of bright yellow, daisy-like flowers. These appear in summer and autumn.

The leaves are lobed.

FIELDS

Yarrow
Achillea millefolium
Daisy family (Asteraceae)

This plant belongs to the Daisy family. It grows to 45 cm tall.

The flowers are small and form the typical flat-topped clusters. They are usually white, but pink flowers are not uncommon.

It has very divided, fern-like leaves.

Spear Thistle
Cirsium vulgare
Daisy family (Asteraceae)

FIELDS

There are many kinds of thistle. The photograph shows the Spear Thistle. This thistle is the emblem of Scotland. The story goes that Scotland was about to be invaded by the Danes. The Danish soldiers took their boots off to creep up on the Scottish soldiers one night, but they stepped onto thistles and their yells woke up the sleeping Scots who managed to chase them off.

It has a large, purple flower. The fluffy seeds are called thistledown and are carried by the wind for long distances. Children often call them fairies and catch them to make a wish.

The leaves are very spiky.

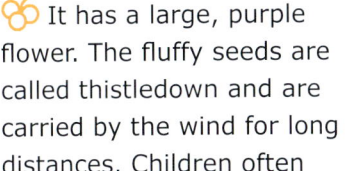

Meadows and Grasslands

Most grassland in Britain is used for grazing or to produce hay for winter fodder. As they are treated with fertiliser to improve grass growth, very few wildflowers will grow here. If left untreated, many more will appear, eventually resulting in beautiful wildflower meadows buzzing with insects. In July grasslands, including meadows, are cut to make hay. By then most wildflowers have produced their seeds which are then left behind when the hay is collected into bales.

Bird's-foot-trefoil

Lotus corniculatus
Pea family (Fabaceae)

This is a member of the Pea family with typical pea flowers.

Flowers are yellow and orange, growing in a loose cluster at the end of the stem. The flowers give the plant its other name of Eggs (the yellow flowers) and Bacon (the orange ones). When the flowers are over, each becomes a tiny pod and the group of pods resembles a bird's foot.

The plant is low growing with small leaves divided into three parts.

Lesser Burdock
Arctium minus
Daisy family (Asteraceae)

This is a large plant growing up to 2 metres tall in summer.

The flowers look like round thistles. The seed heads are covered in hooks and are called burrs. The hooks catch in the fur of passing animals and are carried away to grow in new areas. A hiker noticed how these burrs stuck to his woolly walking socks and was inspired to invent Velcro with its hooks and loops.

It has large, soft, hairy leaves.

Meadow Buttercup
Ranunculus acris
Buttercup family (Ranunculaceae)

There are several kinds of buttercup, actually over 600 worldwide, and all are **poisonous** when eaten. They often grow in damp areas. The one in the photo is the Common or Meadow Buttercup.

They all have flowers with five shiny yellow petals and many stamens. Children often test to see if their friends like butter by holding a flower underneath their chins. If the chin looks yellow, the friend is supposed to like butter… but the yellow is really just the reflection of the shiny petals!

Their leaves are usually divided into three leaflets.

Devil's-bit Scabious
Succisa pratensis
Teasel family (Dipsacaceae)

The name 'Devil's bit' comes from the fact that the root ends suddenly as though it has been bitten off. It grows up to 1 metre high.

It has deep lilac-blue flowers clustered in rounded heads with the stamens sticking up above the petals. The flowers grow on long, hairy stems.

The leaves are long and oval shaped.

Large-flowered Evening-primrose
Oenothera glazioviana
Willowherb family (Onagraceae)

ⓘ As its name suggests, the flowers of Evening-primrose open at night.

🌼 The pale-yellow fragrant flowers attract night-flying moths which pollinate them. The next day the flowers turn orange. They have four petals and are in the Willowherb family.

🌱 The leaves are spear shaped.

Eyebright
Euphrasia nemorosa
Broomrape family (Orobanchaceae)

Eyebright is a plant which grows along the ground. The name Eyebright comes from the fact that it was used in eye medicine in the past.

The tiny, white flowers are very beautiful with purple and yellow markings.

The leaves are oval with deep teeth.

MEADOWS AND GRASSLANDS

Foxglove
Digitalis purpurea
Speedwell family (Veronicaceae)

The Foxglove is a biennial plant which means that it grows for two years. In the first year it only produces a rosette of the large, hairy leaves. The flower spike grows up from this rosette in the second year and can be up to 120 cm tall. Foxgloves are **poisonous**, so be careful not to touch them.

The flowers are usually a deep pink with spots to guide bees to the nectar. You might occasionally find a Foxglove with white flowers.

The large leaves are oval and covered in soft hairs.

Germander Speedwell
Veronica chamaedrys
Speedwell family (Veronicaceae)

(i) There are several species of speedwell but most have bright blue flowers. They are small plants.

> The four petals of Germander Speedwell are white at the centre with dark blue veins and there are only two stamens. The flowers are very short lived.

The leaves grow in pairs and are oval with toothed edges.

MEADOWS AND GRASSLANDS

Wild Pansy
Viola tricolor
Violet family (Violaceae)

(i) Wild Pansy, or Heartease, is much smaller than the garden pansy.

It has small blue, yellow and white flowers with dark lines leading to the centre. These lines are called honey guides as they lead bees to the nectar. The colour of the flowers is very variable – they can be all blue, all yellow or a mixture of colours.

The leaves are long and narrow with extra leafy bits (called stipules) at their bases.

Great Mullein
Verbascum thapsus
Figwort family (Scrophulariaceae)

This is also called Aaron's Rod because of its tall flower spike which can be 1.8 metres in height. This is the height of a tall person.

The flowers are lemon-yellow with five petals and open from the base of the flowering spike.

The leaves are very large and covered in soft hairs.

MEADOWS AND GRASSLANDS

Common Vetch
Vicia sativa
Pea family (Fabaceae)

ⓘ There are many vetch species. The Common Vetch can also be found growing along roadsides and attracts many insect pollinators.

🦋 The purple flowers of Vetch show that it belongs to the Pea family. The seeds are in pods, like tiny pea pods.

🌱 The leaves consist of many paired leaflets with tendrils at the end which curl round nearby stems and allow the plant to scramble up them.

Wild Teasel
Dipsacus fullonum
Teasel family (Dipsacaceae)

Often seen growing at the sides of roads and motorways, Teasel grows up to 2 metres high.

The large flower heads are unusual as the lilac flowers open in a ring around the centre first then further rings of flowers open above and below the first ring. The brown, prickly seed heads persist through the winter and are often collected by flower arrangers.

The large leaves grow in pairs on the stem, joining to make a cup around the stem. They have prickles along the underside of the main vein.

MEADOWS AND GRASSLANDS

Yellow-rattle
Rhinanthus minor
Broomrape family (Orobanchaceae)

Yellow-rattle is a hemi-parasite on grass which means that it gets part of its nutrients from the roots of its grass host. This restricts the growth of the grass so that the wild flowers in the meadow have a better chance of growing well.

The flowers are yellow with an upper and lower lip. The calyx is very inflated with flat sides. When the seeds are ripe they rattle inside the calyx when the wind blows – hence the name Yellow Rattle.

The toothed leaves are long and narrow, growing in pairs on the stem.

Wild Thyme
Thymus drucei
Dead-nettle family (Lamiaceae)

Thyme is a low-growing plant which forms mats on the ground. The whole plant is scented; it is closely related to the herb used in cooking.

It has tiny, purple flowers.

The oval-shaped leaves are also tiny.

MEADOWS AND GRASSLANDS

Common Knapweed
Centaurea nigra
Daisy family (Asteraceae)

(i) Knapweed looks like a thistle without spikes. It grows about 60 cm tall.

The flower buds are brown and scaly, explaining the other name of Hardheads. They open into purple flowers which bees and other insects visit to feed on.

The leaves are long and narrow.

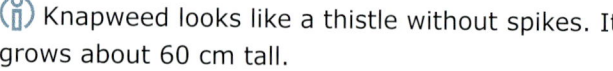

Index

Aaron's Rod 145
Amaranth family 124
Anther 8, 9
Asparagus family 20, 34

Bachelor's Buttons 45
Bedstraw family 100, 105
Bellflower family 43, 45
Bell Heather 46
Bilberry 40
Bindweed family 42, 59, 101
Bird's-foot-trefoil 136
Biting Stonecrop 53
Bittersweet 118
Blackberry 96
Blackthorn 88
Blaeberry 40
Bluebell 19, 20, 43
Borage family 97
Bramble 96
Briar Rose 116
Broad-leaved Dock 98
Broom 38, 39
Broomrape family 141, 148
Bulrush 69
Bulrush family 69
Burdock 137
Butcher's Broom 34
Buttercup 8, 9, 16, 138
Buttercup family 16, 21, 27, 68, 115, 138

Cabbage family 14, 66, 84, 95
Calyx 8, 60, 63, 148
Carpel 9
Carrot family 15, 61, 93, 103, 114
Chickweed 80

Cleavers 100
Clematis 115
Colt's-foot 89
Comfrey 97
Common Cottongrass 41
Common Dog Violet 33
Common Fumitory 94
Common Knapweed 150
Common Vetch 146
Corn Cockle 123
Cornflower 123
Corn Marigold 125
Corn Poppy 10, 129
Cottongrass 41
Cow Parsley 93
Cowslip 90
Crane's-bill 102
Crane's-bill family 102
Crucifer family 14
Cuckooflower 66
Cuckoo Pint 24

Daisy 15, 78, 127
Daisy family 15, 54, 78, 79, 82, 85, 89, 120, 125, 126, 127, 130-133, 137, 150
Daffodil family 22, 26, 32
Dandelion 10, 79
Dead-nettle family 73, 108, 149
Devil's-bit Scabious 139
Dock 98
Dodder 42
Dog-rose 116
Dog's Mercury 23
Dog Violet 33
Dune 57, 58

Eggs and Bacon 136
Elder 99
Enchanter's Nightshade 35

English Stonecrop 53
Evening-primrose 140
Eyebright 141

Fat-hen 124
Fern 49
Fertilisation 9
Field Bindweed 59, 101
Fields 123
Figwort family 145
Filament 8, 9
Fireweed 112
Flower families 14
Fox-and-cubs 85
Foxglove 142
Fumitory 94

Gardens 77
Garlic Mustard 95
Germander Speedwell 143
Gladdon 30
Goosefoot 124
Goosegrass 100
Gorse 38, 39, 42
Grass 10, 41, 135, 148
Grass family 58
Grassland 35
Greater Stitchwort 92
Great Mullein 145
Groundsel 82

Habitat 6, 37, 49, 65
Hardheads 150
Harebell 43
Hawthorn 91
Heartsease 144
Heaths 37
Heather 37, 40, 42, 46
Heather family 40, 46
Hedge Bedstraw 105
Hedge Bindweed 59, 101
Hedge Garlic 95

INDEX

Hedgerows 87
Herb-Robert 102
Hogweed 93, 103
Honey guides 8, 144
Honeysuckle 104
Honeysuckle family 104

Iris family 30, 74
Ivy 121
Ivy family 121
Ivy-leaved Toadflax 51

Jack-by-the-Hedge 95

Kingcup 68
Knapweed 150
Knotweed family 98

Lady's Bedstraw 100, 105
Lady's Smock 66
Lakes 65
Large-flowered Evening-primrose 140
Leaf shapes 11
Lesser Burdock 137
Lesser Periwinkle 107
Lesser Stitchwort 92
Ling 46
Lords-and-Ladies 24
Lords-and-Ladies family 24

Mallow 119
Mallow family 119
Marram 58
Marshes 65
Marsh-marigold 68
May-tree 91
Meadows 135
Meadow Buttercup 138
Meadowsweet 70
Mexican Fleabane 54
Milkwort 44
Milkwort family 44

Moors 37
Moschatel family 99
Mullein 145

Navelwort 50
Nettle 106
Nettle family 52, 106
Nightshade family 118

Old Man's Beard 115
Ovary 8, 9
Ovule 8, 9, 10
Oxeye Daisy 126

Parks 77
Pea family 16, 38, 39, 81, 136, 146
Pellitory-of-the-wall 52
Pennywort 50
Perforate St John's-wort 110
Periwinkle 107
Periwinkle family 107
Petal 8
Petiole 7
Pineappleweed 127
Pink family 29, 60, 67, 80, 92
Pistil 8, 9
Plantain 128
Plantain family 128
Poisonous 6, 15, 24, 98, 104, 113, 118, 131, 138, 142
Pollen 9, 10, 16
Pollination 6, 7, 9, 24
Pollinator 10, 146
Poor Man's Weatherglass 83
Poppy 10, 129
Poppy family 94, 129
Primrose 8, 25, 90
Primrose family 25, 83, 90
Purple-loosestrife 71

Purple-loosestrife family 71

Ragged-Robin 67
Ragwort 131
Ramping-fumitory 94
Ramsons 26
Red Campion 29
Red Clover 81
Red Dead-nettle 108
Red Valerian 55
Reedmace 69
Rhizome 27
Ribwort Plantain 128
Rivers 65
Roadside 26, 52, 85, 87, 146
Rose 14, 116
Rose family 14, 31, 47, 70, 75, 88, 91, 96, 109, 116, 117
Rosebay Willowherb 112
Rowan 109

Scarlet Pimpernel 83
Scentless Mayweed 130
Sea Bindweed 59
Sea Campion 60
Sea-holly 61
Sea-lavender 63
Sea Pink 62
Seashore 57
Sedge 41
Sedge family 41
Sedum 53
Seed Dispersal 10
Sepal 8, 27, 75, 129
Sheep's-bit 45
Shepherd's-purse 84
Sloe 88
Smooth Sowthistle 120
Snapdragon 51, 111
Snowdrop 32
Sowthistle 120
Spathe 24

152

Spadix 24
Spear Thistle 133
Speedwell 143
Speedwell family 51, 111, 142, 143
Spurge family 23
Stamen 8, 9, 16
Sticky Willie 100
Stigma 8, 9, 10, 16
Stinging Nettle 106, 108
Stinking Iris 30
St John's-wort family 110
Stonecrop family 50, 53
Stork's-bill 102
Style 8, 9
Sweet Violet 33

Teasel 147
Teasel family 139, 147
Thrift 62
Thrift family 62, 63
Thyme 149
Toadflax 111

Tormentil 47
Trailing St John's-wort 110
Traveller's-joy 115
Tree Ivy 121

Umbellifer 15, 61, 93
Umbels 15

Valerian family 55
Violet family 33, 144

Walls 49
Water Avens 75
Water-lily family 72
Water Mint 73
White Bryony 113
White Bryony family 113
White Campion 29
White Clover 81
White Dead-nettle 108
White Water-lily 72
Wild Arum 24
Wild Carrot 61, 93, 114

Wild Clematis 115
Wild Daffodil 22
Wild Garlic 26
Wild Pansy 144
Wild Strawberry 117
Wild Teasel 147
Wild Thyme 149
Willowherb family 35, 112, 140
Windflower 27
Wood Anemone 17, 19, 27, 28
Wood Avens 31, 75
Woodlands 19
Wood-sorrel 28
Wood-sorrel family 28
Woody Nightshade 118

Yarrow 132
Yellow Flag 74
Yellow Iris 74
Yellow-rattle 148
Yellow Water-lily 72

Out and About: Discovering British Wild Flowers
Text and images © Deirdre Shirreffs 2021

The author has asserted her rights under the Copyright, Designs and Patents Act 1988 to be identified as the Author of this Work. All Rights Reserved. No part of this book may be reproduced in any form by photocopying or by any electronic or mechanical means, including information, storage or retrieval systems, without permission in writing from both the copyright owners and the publisher of this book.

ISBN 9781908241634

Published 2021 by Brambleby Books, Taunton, Somerset, UK
www.bramblebybooks.co.uk

Book layout by Tanya Warren, Creatix Design
Printed and bound by FINIDR, Czech Rep.

Flower Colour Index

155

Flower Colour Index

157

Flower Colour Index

Useful websites:

xpollination.org/pollipromise/

www.woodlandtrust.org.uk/trees-woods-and-wildlife/plants/wild-flowers

www.plantlife.org.uk/uk/discover-wild-plants-nature/learning-and-volunteering/schools

www.rhs.org.uk/science/conservation-biodiversity/wildlife/plants-for-pollinators

schoolgardening.rhs.org.uk/home

www.growwilduk.com/wildflowers/how-grow-wildflowers

www.wildlifewatch.org.uk

www.rspb.org.uk/fun-and-learning/for-kids

www.activityvillage.co.uk/british-wildlife

www.buglife.org.uk

Other books for children by

Brambleby Books

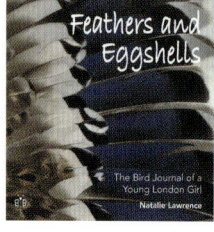

ISBN 9780954334772

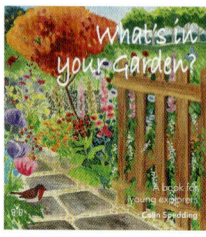

ISBN 9780955392818

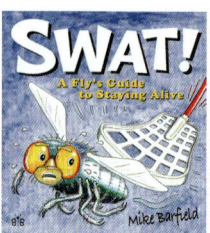

ISBN 9781908241184

ISBN 9781908241443

ISBN 9781908241504

ISBN 9781908241139

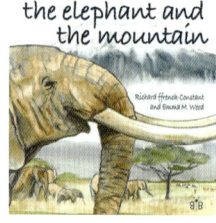

ISBN 9781908241528

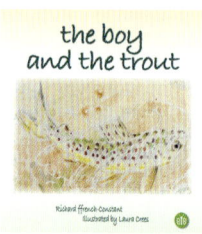

ISBN 9781908241580

ISBN 9781908241573